麻袋后面有几只老鼠?

How many mice are behind the sacks?

XIAOBO HUI SHUSHU LE

小玻会数数了

[英] 艾力克·希尔 著

彭懿 译

接力出版社
Publishing House

爸爸，我能从1数到10了！

Dad, I can count from 1 to 10!

树上有几只松鼠？

How many squirrels are in the tree?

马厩里有几匹马?

How many horses are in the stable?

池塘里有几只鸭子？

How many ducks are on the pond?

猪圈里有几头猪？

How many pigs are in the sty?

院子里有几只母鸡?

How many hens are in the yard?

花园里有几只兔子?

How many rabbits are in the garden?

果园里有几只鹅?

How many geese are in the orchard?

牧场里有几只羊?

How many sheep are in the field?

牛舍里有几头奶牛？

How many cows are in the barn?

桂图登字：20-2007-120

Published by arrangement with Ventura Publishing Limited, a Penguin company.
Original title: SPOT CAN COUNT
Text and illustrations copyright © Eric Hill, 1999
Planned and produced by Ventura Publishing Ltd, 80 Strand, London, WC2 0RL, UK
Eric Hill has asserted his moral rights under the Copyright, Designs and Patents Act 1988.
All rights reserved.

Chinese edition published in 2007 by Jieli Publishing House
The Penguin logo is a registered trademark of Penguin Books Limited

图书在版编目（CIP）数据

小玻会数数了：汉英对照 / （英）希尔著；彭懿译.—南宁：接力出版社，2007.8
书名原文：Spot Can Count
ISBN 978-7-80732-979-4

Ⅰ.小… Ⅱ.①希…②彭… Ⅲ.①英语-汉语-对照读物②图画故事-英国-现代 Ⅳ.H319.4:I

中国版本图书馆 CIP 数据核字（2007）第 122158 号

责任编辑：苗 辉　美术编辑：卢 强
责任校对：张 莉　责任监印：刘 签　版权联络：周梅洁　媒介主理：代 萍
社长：黄 俭　总编辑：白 冰　出版发行：接力出版社
社址：广西南宁市园湖南路 9 号　邮编：530022
电话：0771-5863339（发行部）5866644（总编室）　传真：0771-5863291（发行部）5850435（办公室）
网址：http://www.jielibeijing.com　http://www.jielibook.com　E-mail:jielipub@public.nn.gx.cn

印制：北京华联印刷有限公司
开本：889 毫米×1194 毫米　1/24　印张：1　字数：10 千字
版次：2007 年 9 月第 1 版　印次：2008 年 6 月第 3 次印刷　印数：20 001-30 000 册
定价：13.50 元